I really appreciate how Rebekah combined blessing and declarati... promptings, and prayers given encourage one to be intentional in preparing and praying for oneself and one's baby. One thing I really value in what she has composed is how she provides prayers for baby but as one gets into the second trimester, her prayers are more like promptings so that Mom can listen to the Lord herself and pray for her baby. By the third trimester, she just makes space for Mom to be activated to hear Holy Spirit's heart and prayers for her baby. I believe this book to be a valuable resource for moms to pray, speak life over, prepare, and hear Holy Spirit for the precious life growing inside of them!

- Andrea Bartunek
Mother of five, foster mother of two

This is a great book for anyone who is pregnant! Whether you are ambivalent or excited about your pregnancy, this book offers a raw, vulnerable, and safe place for reflection. It guides a mother into connecting with the heart and spirit of her child. In my career as a home visit nurse for first-time parents in poverty, we talk about the importance of physical nourishment during pregnancy. This book, however, focuses on caring for the heart and soul of the mother, as well as the spirit of the child. Both are of equal importance. I'd recommend this to all newly pregnant families, hands down!

- Mackenzie Hull
Home Visit Nurse with NFP

I love the way there is the option to include my husband in this journal. I feel like he wanted to be more involved in our pregnancy and this helped include him more. The authority and comfort he brought when we would pray together over our baby made me feel supported. It was a good reminder that I wasn't alone. I also love the sections to declare over myself. So often pregnancy is focused on the baby, but it's so good to remember that pregnancy is also a life-changing (and potentially scary) event for the mom! There are so many things that a pregnant mom could worry about, on top of everyone and their mom telling them what they should and should not do during their pregnancy. I love how this journal shifts things towards the positive and brings a calm to the initiation of motherhood. Rebekah lays out prayers to pray; uplifting things to think about; and helps remind us of our authority and the wonderful part we have to play not only in the physical, but also in our babies' spiritual and emotional growth, even from the womb!

- Tiffany Jones
First-time mother

This interactive journal is such a beautiful tool both practically and spiritually for husbands and wives to connect to their new little one or ones. There is so much power and authority when you speak, pray, and declare over someone. Now, to bring this truth into your pregnancy journey as this little life is coming into form, while you partner with the Creator God, is powerful! I think taking time to pause in your day to journal and connect will bring you to an even deeper connection with your baby. I wish I would have had access to such a beautiful journal during my pregnancies. I pray that there will be great life to you and your child from this journal.

- Amy Gagnon
Director of Children's ministry, Bethel Church Redding

We highly recommend *A Precious Life: A Pregnancy Journal to Nurture the Spirit and Soul of You and Your Unborn Child*. Using her personal history, Rebekah delves into concerns that tend to commonly show up during pregnancies and shares truths to victoriously navigate this important season. She addresses common fears around pregnancy and birth, and the book gives outstanding practical wisdom for exercise, nutrition, and expectations for mom and baby. This journal will help you on this path by identifying thoughts, feelings, and goals as you go through pregnancy and birth. All throughout, you will be equipped to develop strong beliefs and Kingdom declarations over your growing family. This is a great resource for expecting parents and new parents.

- Steve & Wendy Backlund
Founders, Igniting Hope Ministries

So, you are pregnant. Being pregnant is a time of exceptional growth for your body as it does stuff it has never done before, but was fully designed to do. This book by Rebekah follows the same metric, but for your spirit. It is designed to teach you the art of engaging with your child's spirit according to your design, and your child's design. I love the fact that Rebekah does not show you how to do it right, but she shows you how to do it according to your own unique design. This is simply beautiful. God has designed your spirit to have a nine-month head start on your soul. You, Mom, are the master craftsman in charge of unpacking the treasures in your child's spirit.

- Arthur Burk
Founder, Sapphire Leadership Group, LLC

A Precious Life

A Pregnancy Journal to Nurture the Spirit and Soul of You and Your Unborn Child

Rebekah Lind

KINGDOM PUBLISHING

Published by Kingdom Publishing
PO Box 630443, Highlands Ranch, CO 80163
www.Kingdom-Publishing.com

This title may be purchased in bulk for educational, business, fund-raising, or sales promotional use. For information, please contact sales@kingdom-publishing.com.

Dedication

I dedicate this book to my two sweet boys. You are my inspiration. I love seeing the fruit in you of the concepts in this book. I look forward to the evidence of the continual manifestation of these truths in your lives. I pray my generation accesses these tools so that your generation may soar on the shoulders of their parents.

Foreword

Dear Reader,

I'm so glad you are holding this book in your hand. I am a midwife, doula, and founder of Fear Birth No More (www.FearBirthNoMore.com). It has always been my passion to empower the everyday couple to a better pregnancy and birth experience.

When I met Rebekah and her husband, Jesse, we connected immediately. I taught them my birthing class in their home and attended the birth of their second child in the role of doula. I had the honor of watching Rebekah be brave amid unexpected and unwanted turns in her labor.

Throughout my time spent with the Lind's, I have noticed their deep intentionality, born from deep love in their hearts for each other and their children. This love has opened their minds to curiosity. They have learned and continue to learn how they can best care for and nurture themselves and their children.

In these pages, Rebekah invites you into that same level of intentionality as you walk through each week of your pregnancy. You, your baby, and your partner are holistic beings, and pregnancy spans the whole of each person involved; spirit, soul, and body. Rebekah has laid out a wonderful template in this journal to help you nurture and connect spiritually, emotionally, and physically with yourself, your baby, and your partner.

I believe this journal will enrich and bless you throughout your pregnancy and even into your parenting!

May you see even more beauty than you already do in this season of life as you work through this journal.

Shannon Lane

Acknowledgements

I want to thank my husband, Jesse, for his support and encouragement and for making time for me to accomplish this project. I love and value you, Sweetheart!

Thanks Mom and Dad for always supporting my dreams.

Thank you to Steve and Wendy Backlund for igniting hope and investing in the beliefs of the body of Christ. Your ministry has had great transformational impact on my life.

Thank you, Arthur Burk, for investing in the body of Christ through your spiritual journey. The tools and teaching you've made available are invaluable.

Thank you, Christine Tracy, for editing, answering my questions, and supporting this dream.

Thank you, Anne Thompson, for believing in this book. I've felt your support for me as a mom first and then as an author, which I greatly value.

Thank you, Tracy Fagan, for helping me make this book a published reality.

Table of Contents

Introduction

Welcome to one of the most amazing adventures of your life! Congratulations on your pregnancy. I'm so excited for you!

My heart behind writing this pregnancy journal is: to create a space for you to make time to think, reflect, and meditate on what it means to nurture your baby during pregnancy; to help you begin preparing yourself for this little life to enter your everyday life in such an incredible way; and to encourage you to take time not only to think about how you're nourishing yourself and your baby physically, but also emotionally and spiritually.

I think it's so easy to get caught up in all of the physical changes and making sure that you're doing everything you can to help this little one grow healthy and strong inside of you. But we sometimes tend to forget that he/she has a spirit and that we have the opportunity as parents to nurture his/her spirit throughout the entire pregnancy. We are able to give our baby's spirit a nine-month head start over their soul and body. Let's take advantage of that.

I'm writing this journal during my second pregnancy because I worked through a pregnancy journal during my first pregnancy, and although I enjoyed it, I felt it was missing the important component of nurturing the spirit of my little one and I would have liked everything to be in one resource. So, here you are.

I've incorporated resources and concepts I learned from Arthur Burk about the importance of blessing your child's spirit throughout the nine months of pregnancy, as well as those from Terry and Jackie Mize about the importance of biblical declarations over your body and all the phases of pregnancy. You can buy their books and teachings for further development of these concepts and begin to write your own declarations and blessings as you become familiar with how it's done. I've written some of each at the beginning to get you started, but then I began to leave those places blank each week to allow you to personalize them even more, based on your needs and desires.

My hope is that you will use this journal to launch into your own prayers, thoughts, and learning about pregnancy and this sweet life you get to nurture and raise. I encourage you not to let it become a stress, pressure, or "to do" task, but rather a special time each week to sit down, relax, and be with the Lord and your baby. If you don't know how to fill something out, leave it blank or come back later when you want to answer it. Most of all, ENJOY!

A Word to Dads/Husbands

You have an incredible opportunity to nurture your child and your wife/partner throughout this pregnancy too! Although you're not physically carrying the baby and probably won't feel as connected to the child during this phase, you can begin to be intentional about nurturing a connection with your baby by participating in blessing your baby's spirit and declaring truth and revelation for their soul, as well as helping your wife/partner feel emotionally and spiritually supported through this time of huge change for her. There are very important things that only men/dads can impart to their children, because you as a male represent a very specific part of our Heavenly Father's heart that women simply cannot bring to their child in the same way.

While pregnant with both of my two boys, I wanted my husband to be more involved. But I had to work hard to try to communicate what I was hoping to receive from him, and how I desired for him to be involved in our boys' lives while they were still inside of me. I knew he was fully invested in each pregnancy and desired to be a wonderful father, but he didn't always know how to do that and needed my guidance. I had to talk to him about how I was feeling, or what was developing in the baby that week. Other times I asked him to pray for or bless my body in a particularly uncomfortable time. Still other times we joined together in praying blessings for our baby.

I want to encourage you to be intentional with your wife/partner and baby during this pregnancy. Ask Holy Spirit how to support her, and ask your wife/partner to communicate what she hopes you will do to support her. Holy Spirit and your wife/partner are the best at knowing what she needs.

God has entrusted you with this child, so He wants to help guide you in raising him/her from the moment of conception. You've been given the tools you need and where you feel lacking, look for resources or other fathers who have gone before you. You were made for this, so you can be successful at it even in the midst of failures. God is behind you and for you!

How to Use This Journal

The first section is sometimes lighthearted and sometimes deeper. Fill in the blank or circle the appropriate response. It's pretty self-explanatory. I have intentionally left space around all forward slash options (Eg: his / her; Myself / My Wife; Prayer / Blessing / Scripture etc.) so that you can circle the appropriate choice for your situation.

The *"What I'm Thinking About This Week"* section is really just for your own notes or for journaling your thoughts. Don't feel pressured to fill it out every week, but it's my way of giving you your own space to write things down or to note the first time you feel baby kick (because it happens at different weeks for everyone during each pregnancy); or to note things you may be struggling with or having victory in as far as your thoughts, health, feelings, and family.

The *"My Prayer/Blessing/Word for You This Week"* section is specifically to focus on your baby's spiritual and emotional development. For the first 20 weeks I've given you specific blessings, Scriptures, etc., to declare and pray for your baby. For the next 10 weeks I've given you prompts from which to write your own. For the final 10 weeks I've left blank lines to encourage you to seek the Lord as to what to bless, prophesy, and declare for your child as they near their time to enter the world. Enjoy this process and perhaps use it as quiet time once a week because it's a process with the Lord and He wants to be intimately involved with this part of your life.

The *"Declaration for Myself/My Wife for This Pregnancy"* section is designed for you and/or your husband/ the dad to make declarations over your pregnancy that bring life and health to your spirit, soul, and body. It will help you choose hope and God's best for you even when there may be times of struggle and discomfort. Choosing to agree with God's Word and truth for you is a powerful tool to keep hope alive and not allow the enemy's lies to penetrate your heart or affect you.

For some of us, the lines left to fill in will be just enough space. For some, they may feel overwhelmingly too much, and for others not nearly enough for all we want to say. We all have different ways of communicating so I want to encourage you to make this journal your own. If you need more space to write your thoughts, then staple in extra sheets of paper with your thoughts and scribbles on that week's page(s). If you feel like you can't fill the lines, don't worry about it. If you have little doodles or other creative ideas (drawings, poems, paintings, collages etc.) while you're spending time each week, staple them into the book or take a picture to print and staple if it's too big to fit in the journal. Everyone's journal should be uniquely theirs and tell their story in a special way. This may end up being a special keepsake/memoir to pass on to your children later in life, so I hope you will use it to begin to build principles for a strong spiritual and emotional legacy for your family.

The *"Did You Know?"* section is not meant to be used as medical advice. It includes information I've learned from my community team during both of my pregnancies; people such as my chiropractor, homebirth midwife, naturopath, oils specialist, Pilates instructor, and doula. It's been my experience that much of this information is not known or shared by most OB/GYN or hospital-based midwives, thus I've included it in hopes that it will be helpful and perhaps inspire further research. If nothing else, it's interesting, fascinating information that points to our amazing Creator and His design for life.

Medical Disclaimer: *Information and advice given in this book should not be used as medical advice in place of a medical professional. It is only presented as information learned and found to be helpful by the author. Please seek a healthcare professional before taking or applying any of the advice herein. The author takes no responsibility and is not liable for anything a reader does with this information outside of the advice and care of a healthcare professional.*

My First Pregnancy

My husband and I are both the oldest of five, and we both to this day have great relationships with our siblings. Consequently, when we got married, we both desired to have four to six children. We were in our early 30s by the time we found each other and married, so although we wanted to have some "just us" time before having children, we didn't want to wait too long with body clock stuff...(although God has reminded me many times that He can give me the desires of my heart regardless of what society says about how old or young you should be to have children).

We had been married a little over a year before we started trying, but we ran into unexpected delays and difficulty getting pregnant. It took us 2.5 years before we conceived, but that's a story for another time. We were of course over the moon when we found out we were pregnant and there were a lot of tears of joy among family members as we shared our God news!

My pregnancy was going smoothly (no morning sickness and no other negative symptoms and I was feeling great) when at 18 weeks we found out I had several very large fibroids which were causing me to present almost as if I were carrying twins. I was in an incredible amount of pain; had difficulty eating; and was stuck to my bed or the couch except to use the restroom. It was a difficult time emotionally and spiritually because we feared early onset labor and were also concerned the baby would have difficulty growing due to the size of the fibroids in my uterus.

My dream of a home birth was pretty much eliminated as an option short of a miracle because of an overall fear for my baby's life. I thank God for my family who looked after me during the days my husband was working as I couldn't really care for myself. Their prayers, encouragement, and faith kept me going and focused on God's promises for my baby's life. I was in this state, icing my belly to keep inflammation at bay (20 minutes on and 20 minutes off around the clock) for six weeks and had to leave all of my part-time jobs for the remainder of my pregnancy. During this time, I wrestled with God, not understanding why this was happening to me. I tried to believe for His healing, remain hopeful and in faith, not giving in to fear.

Although we tried everything to turn my son, he remained in a breech position from around week 30, due to what we believe were the fibroids being in the way of his moving. A Caesarean section was inevitable, according to doctors. I wrestled with the Lord about why He didn't just turn my son for me so I could deliver him vaginally. After doing monthly ultrasounds to check baby's development; trying my best not to over-exert myself; and praying a ton; I went into labor a week early. I was relieved and thankful to go into labor naturally because now I at least knew what it felt like. My son was delivered safely by C-section after about 17 hours of labor. He was perfect and healthy, and despite being tired from loss of blood during the procedure, I was doing well.

Although I didn't get the answers I wanted, I did choose faith and to believe that God is still good and redeems all things. About two months after my son was born, I sought help from a naturopath to deal with the fibroids. After what felt like a long 18 months of supplements, dietary adjustments, prayer, and heart healing, we had an ultrasound showing all fibroids were gone. We felt released to start trying for our second baby.

This time we got pregnant immediately, which was an answer to prayer and somewhat of a surprise at God's goodness. I think I was hesitant to believe we would conceive that quickly. I felt cautious about dealing with disappointment again, like I'd done for so long during our trying period with our first. I knew God could change things and honestly believed we'd taken care of some spiritual things that had been blocking our ability to conceive the first time. But fear of being disappointed again was still lurking in the back of my mind. I am so thankful that God came through and proved His goodness and faithfulness to us yet again. I never want to lose the wonder and awe I have for Him in this.

My Second Pregnancy

When I got pregnant the second time, I had a different and much better experience in a lot of ways. I experienced morning sickness this time around, and as I continued to declare that I did not have to experience this symptom to have a healthy pregnancy, it did get better. I also couldn't help but wonder if the Lord allowed it as a sign that my hormones were doing better and as a way for Him to begin speaking to me about His redemption of this pregnancy. Throughout my second pregnancy, the Lord spoke and confirmed that He was redeeming pregnancy for me in so many ways. Overall, I had a very easy pregnancy; not too many difficult symptoms. The hardest part was the decreased capacity to participate in outside activities. I have had a tendency to be an overachiever in life and I had to adjust my expectations of myself so I could prioritize nurturing the little life inside of me.

When we went in for our 20-week ultrasound, they discovered one small fibroid in an insignificant location; and the baby was growing normally and very healthy. The fibroid news could have knocked my faith to the ground, but instead I felt strong and kept hope. I didn't give it influence to allow fear and worry into my thoughts. We started appropriate treatment with our naturopath in order to support my body in eliminating this fibroid, and the 28-week ultrasound revealed it had not been eliminated but also hadn't grown. We took that as a win and continued supporting my body with supplements and dietary choices to minimize growth.

The birth of baby number two did not go as I had desired, with some hormone imbalance restraining my body from responding as it should to the contractions, thus requiring much more intervention. Ultimately, we were able to deliver by VBAC (vaginal birth after cesarean) and both baby and I were healthy.

I got my vaginal delivery, which was a huge answer to prayer, and I will continue to do my heart work and support my body well nutritionally, partnering with and believing God for glory to glory and strength to strength in each of my next pregnancies. I hope you can learn from my story, and through using this book, to stand powerfully in your authority as a daughter of the King of Kings, which will in turn bless your baby tremendously.

This book, A Precious Life, is a result of joy-filled, Spirit-inspired, grace-empowered writing throughout this pregnancy. I've always desired to write books, but this, my first, came from my adventures with the Lord during my own pregnancies. I sat down throughout this pregnancy and would invite the Holy Spirit to direct my words and they would flow so easily. I'm excited to watch how the Lord partners with me in blessing you and your children as you work through this book with Him during these precious nine months. May His blessings and favor be upon you and your family!

Your Journey Begins

Weeks 4-6

I just found out you're on your way, my precious little _____. (Week _____)

I can / can't believe I get to be your mom!

My first thought when I found out I was pregnant with you was: _____

_____

_____

_____

_____

Cravings so far:_____

_____

_____

Morning Sickness/Other symptoms: _____

_____

_____

_____

What I'm Thinking About This Week is: _____

_____

_____

_____

_____

_____

_____

A Precious Life: A Pregnancy Journal to Nurture the

My Prayer / Blessing / Word for You This Week is:

Baby, God has thought of you since the creation of the world and He wanted Mommy and Daddy to conceive you right at this time in history because He has specific plans and purposes for you to fulfill. I bless your spirit and soul to know that you have a destiny and dreams and desires that God has created you with that He wants to partner with you in bringing to fulfillment. He calls you beautiful/handsome, smart, unique, strong, courageous, and intelligent and believes in you for always. I bless your spirit with knowing these truths innately and with the ability to lead your soul and body in acting on this truth through the entirety of your life.

Declaration for Myself / My Wife for This Pregnancy:

I declare this pregnancy will carry through to full term with no complications and no fear. This baby has a destiny and the Lord has a plan and purpose that does *not* involve miscarriage. So I choose to ignore any fears of that and focus on His plan for this little one. (Repeat this as often as you need to in order to keep your heart and mind staid on God's plan for your pregnancy. You are powerful and can take authority over your body and your baby.)

Week 7

My chosen form of exercise for this pregnancy is:

- ○ Walking
- ○ Swimming
- ○ Lifting weights
- ○ Pilates
- ○ Running
- ○ Dancing
- ○ Other: _____

We've decided to tell our families about this little one when: _____

_____

_____

One of the things your dad and I have been talking about when we think of you is: _____

_____

_____

_____

_____

_____

What I'm Thinking About This Week is: _____

_____

_____

_____

_____

_____

_____

_____

My Prayer / Blessing / Word for You This Week is:

My sweet one, I declare that you bring hope and life wherever you go, even now in my womb! I call your spirit to attention and I bless your spirit to lead your body in perfect development in every way throughout this entire nine months in my womb. I bless your eyes to see perfectly, 20/20 or better; your ears to hear excellently; your bones and teeth to develop to be strong and healthy; your brain, spine and nervous system to function perfectly in tandem to maintain perfect development and health for your whole body all the days of your life. I bless your genes to be inherited only as the Kingdom of God would intend without broken pieces or family history beliefs that would curse you with disease or fear. I declare you are developing perfectly in spirit, soul, and body, and I place a hedge of protection from the Lord over your growth and development so there are *no* disruptions or hiccups of any kind during this pregnancy or afterwards.

Declaration for Myself / My Wife for This Pregnancy:

I declare that my body will receive the good food that I am feeding it and that it will process, metabolize, and absorb all the nutrients for myself and my baby. I bless my body to process all the hormones it is producing right now appropriately and to only produce what is needed for a healthy pregnancy and development of my baby. I bless my liver to function perfectly in every way. I bless my sense of smell to work for me and not against me in helping me choose foods that are nutritious and will provide strength and energy for me and my little one. I bless my stomach to keep down all of the food I put into it and to remain settled at all times. I declare that I can experience a healthy pregnancy without morning sickness, in Jesus' name.

Did You Know?

Running during pregnancy, especially during your third trimester, puts undue pressure on your pelvic floor muscles. Consider how this will impact your body later in life before you try to prove you can run through your whole pregnancy. It's not about whether you can, but whether you should. (See a pelvic floor physical therapist or women's health physical therapist for more info.)

[Rachel Algra, Polestar Pilates Practitioner, https://taylorpilatesandfitness.com/about-us/instructors/, 2019]

Week 8

Decisions and Reflections

We're deciding where we want to bring you into the world. So far, our plan is to deliver you at:

- ○ The hospital
- ○ A birthing center
- ○ Home
- ○ Other _____
- ○ We don't know yet.

It's Summer / Fall / Winter / Spring right now so one of the ways I'm spending time reflecting on and thinking of you is by: _____

_____

_____

_____

_____

_____

Think for a moment about how you are feeling, as the mother of this child, about this pregnancy so far. If you could put movement or a dance to your feelings or thoughts, what would it look like? (Jumping up and down; slow and graceful; a jig?) _____

_____

_____

_____

_____

_____

Go ahead and do that movement. It'll be fun! Release that feeling as you do it.

What I'm Thinking About This Week is: _____

_____

_____

_____

_____

_____

_____

_____

_____

_____

_____

My Prayer / Blessing / Word for You This Week is:

My precious baby, I bless your growth and development to continue to proceed normally in every way. I bless your spirit to grow daily in the knowledge of the presence of God all around you and His incredible love for you. I bless your soul to sense and receive your dad's and my love for you as unconditional and forever because that is our intention toward you. Even as we're adjusting to the idea that you're coming into our life, we are excited and desire to be the best parents we can be to you. We choose to trust Holy Spirit inside of us to guide and direct us in guiding you into all that He's created and desires for you to be. We continue to bless your spirit to lead you in every aspect of your life as your spirit is led by Holy Spirit!

Declaration for Myself / My Wife for This Pregnancy:

Body, I speak to you and I bless you to receive rest and refreshment as I sleep at night and during naps. I bless you to sluff off stress and receive the peace that passes understanding that Jesus promises to give us as our inheritance in Him. I bless you to maintain healthy energy levels throughout this pregnancy and to impart peace and rest to my baby as well. Soul/heart, I speak to you and give you permission to take the mental and emotional time to maintain peace and to rest appropriately for this season. You are not lazy or weak. You are courageous and strong and bold and I am proud of the mother you are preparing to be. I bless you with grace and fresh strength for each day, offered to you directly from the Lord. Receive it daily!

Week 9

- ○ I can hardly wait until...
- ○ I am looking forward to...
- ○ I am hoping to put off...
- ○ I am anxious about...

... when I begin to start showing. This is mostly because: _____

_____

_____

_____

_____

I had a funny / interesting / scary thought this week: _____

_____

_____

_____

_____

_____

If you were to create a logo to represent your baby, what would it look like? Draw, sketch or doodle your ideas here:

What I'm Thinking About This Week is: _____

_____

_____

_____

_____

_____

_____

_____

_____

_____

_____

_____

_____

My Prayer / Blessing / Word for You This Week is:

My sweetie pie, I call your spirit to attention in the name of Jesus of Nazareth. Listen with your spirit to God's Word for you. Psalms 139:13-16 says, *"For you created my inmost being; you knit me together in my mother's womb. I praise you because I am fearfully and wonderfully made; your works are wonderful, I know that full well. My frame was not hidden from you when I was made in the secret place, when I was woven together in the depths of the earth. Your eyes saw my unformed body; all the days ordained for me were written in your book before one of them came to be"* (NIV). I bless your senses, my sweet child, to develop fully and with perfect function so that you may fully experience life in the way God intended. I declare you will have perfect vision, regardless of what my or your dad's genes "should" dictate. I bless you with perfect hearing, taste, feel, and smell as well so that each of these senses may add an element to your understanding of who God is and His beauty all around you. I also bless your spiritual senses to develop with the presence of God as your baseline so that you may use the resources God has given you to partner well with Him.

Declaration for Myself / My Wife for This Pregnancy:

I bless my body to remain strong and healthy and symptom-free from anything negative throughout the entirety of my pregnancy. I bless my body to adjust appropriately to the new weight I'm carrying; that my muscles would strengthen correctly as needed so I do not experience hemorrhoids, back or round ligament pain, SI (sacroiliac joint) pain, or anything else. I bless my digestion to continue normally without experiencing heartburn or constipation. I bless my sleep to be deep, uninterrupted, and peaceful throughout my entire pregnancy. I bless my body to receive all my water intake and use it where needed rather than storing it unnecessarily and causing swelling in my hands, feet, or any other area of my body. I bless my blood pressure to stay within normal levels throughout my whole pregnancy. I refuse to give fear of labor or delivery any place in my mind or heart. I choose to believe that my body was created to conceive, carry to full term, and deliver my precious baby with no complications, and I give myself permission to dwell on this truth and trust my body to do what it was created to do.

Did You Know?

A high protein diet in pregnancy (80-120g/day) is essential for building your blood volume, for baby's development, and the development of uterine tissue and the placenta. It can eliminate the risk of many "common" issues women face in pregnancy today.

(Check out www.therealblueribbonbaby.org for more information)

[Jan Lapetino CPM, RM & Maren Wood CPM, RM, *Homebirth: A Midwife's Guide for Parents*, Denver, CO, 2011, pg. 19-22]

Reflections

_____

_____

_____

_____

_____

_____

_____

_____

_____

_____

_____

_____

_____

_____

_____

_____

_____

_____

_____

_____

_____

_____

Week 10

I can't believe you've been growing inside me for 10 weeks now.

- ○ I've dreamed about this my whole life.
- ○ I never really thought about what it would be like.
- ○ I wondered if I'd ever have this experience of pregnancy.
- ○ I always imagined it would be very different than it has been.
- ○ Other: _____

_____

_____

I feel _____ about the first time I will feel you move inside of me.

Maybe it will be like: _____

or maybe I'll notice: _____

or maybe it won't be like anyone has described it. Will it feel the same as my last pregnancy?

Regardless of how it feels, I look forward to that part of this experience.

What I'm Thinking About This Week is: _____

_____

_____

_____

_____

_____

_____

_____

_____

My Prayer / Blessing / Word for You This Week is:

Sweet baby of mine, I call your spirit to attention to listen and receive the truth of God for you! God is currently creating your innermost being with desires and dreams and destiny and thoughts that He wants to see come into fulfillment. He is knitting you together in Mommy's womb; every cell is perfectly formed and connected to function the way He's created the human body to be created and function. You are fearfully and wonderfully made because that's how God has chosen to make you. He has chosen your chromosomes, your genes, your family heritage, your mom and dad and siblings; all on purpose. You are a gift, a blessing, a precious child to Him and to your dad and me! You are not hidden except for protection for a season. You are known and desired and wanted. Your heavenly Father watches over you every second of every day. Know and receive this as ultimate truth.

Declaration for Myself / My Wife for This Pregnancy:

I declare that my placenta will fully form and develop to provide everything my baby needs throughout this entire pregnancy. I bless it to be located in an optimal, safe location within my uterus so as not to create any fear or complications. I bless my uterus, the amniotic sac, my placenta and all other essential parts that are needed to sustain this pregnancy to full term. I bless each part of the system to function in full health exactly the way God created each to function in order to sustain this life inside of me until he/she is ready to enter the world. I speak peace from Heaven over my mind and heart as I converse with medical professionals and moms, etc., around this pregnancy so that I can easily receive truth and flush lies or fears that are not part of my birthright as a Kingdom believer. I declare that I will focus only on what is God's best for me and this baby and believe His promises to His children concerning our health and our inheritance.

Week 11

I've been thinking about _____ recently and wondering how I will tell you

_____.

My thoughts are overflowing with _____ towards you! If I could tell

you anything right now as I looked into your eyes it would be: _____

_____

_____

_____

_____

_____

The color that best describes my feelings / thoughts around this pregnancy so far is: _____

_____

_____

The reason for this color is: _____

_____

_____

_____

What I'm Thinking About This Week is: _____

_____

_____

_____

_____

_____

_____

A Precious Life: A Pregnancy Journal to Nurture the

My Prayer / Blessing / Word for You This Week is:

My powerful one, I call your spirit to attention and I bless your spirit to lead your soul and body in listening and receiving the truth of God's Word for your life. You have been made in the image of God to take dominion over the earth and rule as God's partner in bringing His Kingdom to earth so that it looks like Heaven. You are powerful and anointed and equipped with everything you need to lead and to accomplish His purposes and your dreams in this lifetime. I bless you to know in your spirit that you've been created and born for such a time as this. You have choices and have been given discernment and wisdom for your assignment. Nothing can come against you because God is on your side and you are covered under His wings of grace, favor, and protection. I bless you to know His safety and security all the days of your life and to dwell in His heart and His presence increasingly every day.

Declaration for Myself / My Wife for This Pregnancy:

I bless and declare that my body is healthy and whole and that within it exists everything to maintain this health and wholeness while also nurturing the baby in my womb. I declare that my senses will be attuned to the Spirit in every aspect of my life including how to nurture this baby spiritually, mentally, and physically. I declare that my transition into motherhood or having multiple children will be smooth and graceful. God will give me everything I need - patience, gentleness, courage, and consistency - to be the best mother I can be.

Did You Know?

Doing Kegels regularly throughout your pregnancy can assist you in quicker healing after birth, less trauma to your pelvic floor during childbirth, and greater bladder control post birth. It's essential to a woman's health. (See a women's health professional for details.)

[Jan Lapetino CPM, RM & Maren Wood CPM, RM, *Homebirth: A Midwife's Guide for Parents*, Denver, CO, 2011, pg. 29]

Week 12

I have a strong sense that you are a

- ○ Boy
- ○ Girl
- ○ I don't have a sense one way or the other.

The thing I'm enjoying most about this pregnancy right now is: _____

_____

_____

What do you imagine your baby looks like as he/she moves inside of you? During this week, put some music on and move/dance with your baby. Imagine your baby moving with you as the Holy Spirit inspires your movement. Dance like no one is watching! Write something about this experience here: _____

_____

_____

_____

_____

What I'm Thinking About This Week is: _____

_____

_____

_____

_____

_____

_____

_____

My Prayer / Blessing / Word for You This Week is:

Precious baby, I bless your spirit to receive the word of the Lord for your life. Ephesians 2:10: *"For we are God's handiwork, created in Christ Jesus to do good works, which God prepared in advance for us to do"* (NIV). You are God's masterpiece, His poetry, His dance, His representation of Himself on earth. You were designed with purpose, not only His, but yours as well and these work together to impact and change the world around you. I bless you to know your purpose in Him and to see the fulfillment of this purpose throughout your life. You carry a piece of the puzzle of life, a unique voice, a specific set of skills, that no one else has or can bring in the capacity that you can. The world would be missing a part of God without your existence. I bless you to know and operate from this sense of significance throughout your whole life; for it to be a belief ingrained in the very fibers of your being!

Declaration for Myself / My Wife for This Pregnancy:

I declare that as I near the end of my first trimester that I will continue from glory to glory and strength to strength in my physical, mental, and spiritual capacity to carry this child. In turn I will be an encouragement and a blessing to other mamas around me to stand firm in their Kingdom authority over their bodies and pregnancies. I declare that pregnancy is a blessing and a normal part of life; that it doesn't need to be a medical condition or a setback or restraint on what God is doing in and through me. I declare that although it is a preparation period for me and my baby, it is not an end to life as I know it and will not hinder me from accomplishing the dreams and desires God has placed in my heart to do. I declare God has given me the strength and grace to function fully in every role He's given me: wife, friend, daughter, mother, employee, leader (fill in the blanks).

Week 13

So far, my eating habits with this pregnancy are:

○ Perfect, I'm being careful to eat enough protein, eat regularly, and never touch sugar.
○ Pretty good, I'm eating mostly healthy but definitely giving in to cravings that aren't great sometimes.
○ I'm eating anything and everything I can get my hands on; I'm always starving!
○ Not great, this is an area I'd like to work on, but it's been hard with not feeling well.
○ Other: _____

We're at the end of our first trimester my sweetie pie! We only have two more to go and I'm looking forward to getting to know you more over the next six months even before I get to look you in the eyes and tell you: _____

_____

_____

_____

○ I've thought of a nickname for you. It is_____
○ I have not thought of a nickname for you because I'm waiting to find out your gender.

What I'm Thinking About This Week is: _____

_____

_____

_____

_____

_____

_____

_____

_____

_____

_____

My Prayer / Blessing / Word for You This Week is:

My sweet one, I call your spirit to attention to listen to God's truth for you. *"But why am I so favored, that the mother of my Lord should come to me? As soon as the sound of your greeting reached my ears, the baby in my womb leaped for joy. Blessed is she who has believed that the Lord would fulfill his promises to her!"* (Luke 1:43-45, NIV). Baby, I bless you to know that you are highly favored, and you have been created with the ability to recognize life and those giving life to you. You have the ability to exchange life-giving energy with those around you, not only to give but to receive life and give great blessings of peace and joy to others as well. Favor goes before you and follows you wherever you go and will always be upon you because the Lord is upon you and has anointed you to do good deeds for His glory. You are blessed beyond belief and thus you can bless others with what God has given you. I bless you to be filled with faith and to believe God in every situation so that your agreement with Him will bring things to pass in your lifetime that wouldn't otherwise be fulfilled. I bless you to be known as a woman or man of faith; one who believes God at His word regardless of what the circumstances or situations seem to dictate.

Declaration for Myself / My Wife for This Pregnancy:

I declare in this season of unique God-given life growing within my womb, that I will continue to have the necessary energy and stamina to accomplish the things He's put in my hands to do, while also receiving His grace for the changing season. I let go of unreasonable expectations, mine and those others put on me, and I press in to what it looks like to adjust to and accomplish His expectations: receiving His love, basking in His presence, knowing and being known by Him. I come into agreement with His goodness that is always aimed at me, and I receive His grace to be fully content in this season, completely enjoying being present in each moment of this pregnancy.

Did You Know?

Have you heard of diastasis recti? Many women's rectus abdominis muscles separate during pregnancy to make room for their baby. To avoid delaying or preventing correct natural healing of these muscles after pregnancy, avoid planking, sit-ups and other such abdominal work that results in your abs looking like a tent when doing them. (Research your local Polestar Pilates Practitioners for safe abdominal exercises during pregnancy or see a Women's Health Physical Therapist.)

[Rachel Algra, Polestar Pilates Practitioner, https://taylorpilatesandfitness.com/about-us/instructors/, 2019]

Week 14

I feel:

- ○ Relieved
- ○ Nervous
- ○ Excited
- ○ Surprised
- ○ Other: _____

- to have reached my second trimester.

What I did to intentionally talk to / spend time with you this week was: _____

_____

_____

_____

_____

As you ask the Lord, what color does He bring to mind that represents your baby? Use this color to doodle below as you pray for your baby and ask God what that color represents about your little one.

What I'm Thinking About This Week is: _____

_____

_____

_____

_____

_____

My Prayer / Blessing / Word for You This Week is:

My precious sweetie pie, I bless you with Philippians 2:1: *"Look at how much encouragement you've found in your relationship with the Anointed One! You are filled to overflowing with his comforting love. You have experienced a deepening friendship with the Holy Spirit and have felt his tender affection and mercy"* (TPT). I bless you to always know and receive encouragement and comfort in your relationship with Jesus and to turn to Him in every situation where you feel unsure or uncertain of what to do or how to respond. I bless you to overflow with His wrap-around presence and to feel His deep comforting arms of love surrounding you. He will always carry the answer, the courage, and the strength that you need. I bless your relationship with Jesus and Holy Spirit to be continually developing and deepening from this day forward. I bless you to be aware of and intensely experience His tender affection, mercy, and grace over every aspect of your life. I bless you to see His gaze of fierce love as He looks into your eyes and to see yourself as the beauty He sees when He looks at you!

Declaration for Myself / My Wife for This Pregnancy:

I agree with Proverbs 3:24 that *"[I] will sleep like a baby, safe and sound— [my] rest will be sweet and secure"* (TPT, author's emphasis), throughout the rest of this pregnancy! I declare that as I seek the Lord, He hears me and delivers me from all fear that tries to take hold around medical advice, people's experiences, or anything else that would hinder me from receiving and resting in God's peace for this pregnancy (see Psalms 34:4). I declare that I will live with the 2 Corinthians 10:5 mindset over this pregnancy, which says: *"I can demolish every deceptive fantasy that opposes God and break through every arrogant attitude that is raised up in defiance of the true knowledge of God. I will capture, like prisoners of war, every thought and insist that it bow in obedience to the Anointed One"* (excerpted from TPT). I am powerful and what I choose to believe and dwell on comes into being and dictates a lot of my experience and overall feeling about this pregnancy. So, when I align my thoughts with God's Word and choose to believe Him at His Word, it makes a difference. This pregnancy will proceed normally and, in every way, healthy from here on out, in Jesus' name.

Spirit and Soul of You and Your Unborn Child

Week 15

We have:

- ○ Decided to find out the gender of this baby.
- ○ Decided not to find out the gender of this baby.
- ○ Not decided which way to go yet.

One of the new things I'm experiencing in my body this week / recently is _____

_____

_____

_____

_____

What image does God show you when you ask Him about your baby? It could be a flower, object, landscape; the ideas are endless. Don't be intimidated or shut down your creativity. Flow with the process and draw or sketch it below:

What I'm Thinking About This Week is: _____

_____

_____

_____

_____

_____

_____

My Prayer / Blessing / Word for You This Week is:

My precious little one, I call your spirit to attention in the name of Jesus and I bless your spirit to receive the word of the Lord for you. Nehemiah 8:10: *"He continued, 'Go home and prepare a feast, holiday food and drink; and share it with those who don't have anything: This day is holy to God. Don't feel bad. The joy of God is your strength!' (The Message)."* I bless you to always have more than enough because God is your provider, so that you may share with those who have nothing. I bless you to live in such a way that every day is holy to God and to live with a healthy fear of God all your days so that you may truly know Him. I bless you to know when to grieve and when to rejoice and how to process your emotions effectively so as to allow your soul to remain healthy and your focus to always be on God's goodness! His goodness never changes no matter the circumstances, so I bless you to know, believe, and receive this truth daily. I bless you to know and remember in every circumstance that the Lord's joy is your strength and you always have access to it from within. You may grieve and feel opposite emotions to joy and yet still draw strength from His joy! I bless and seal these truths in your spirit.

Declaration for Myself / My Wife for This Pregnancy:

"Stop imitating the ideals and opinions of the culture around you; but be inwardly transformed by the Holy Spirit through a total reformation of how you think. This will empower you to discern God's will as you live a beautiful life, satisfying and perfect in his eyes" (Romans 12:2, TPT). I declare that I surrender to Holy Spirit's transformation of me and reformation of how I think about life so that He may not only teach me what to think and how to view this pregnancy, but that this transformation will also translate to how I parent, train, love, and nurture this child into his/her God-given talents and anointings. I declare that this pregnancy will be beautiful, satisfying, and perfect in my eyes and the Lord's and that I am empowered to discern God's will throughout this journey of pregnancy and into parenting.

Did You Know?

Taking fish oil during pregnancy and breastfeeding can significantly help prevent what's commonly called "mommy brain." Growing and nursing a baby takes significantly more DHA and EPA, which are Omega 3's ('healthy brain fats'). Your body is designed to give baby what he/she needs first, so you can often feel fuzzy-headed and have a hard time thinking, remembering, or bringing words to mind when you are low on this important nutrition. I recommend Nordic Naturals brand Complete Omega because this has high enough levels of EPA and DHA for pregnancy and the oil doesn't go rancid like many capsules do.

[Dr. Patti Gonzalez, D.C. http://www.yourhealthelevated.com, 2016]

Reflections

_____
_____
_____
_____
_____
_____
_____
_____
_____
_____
_____
_____
_____
_____
_____
_____
_____
_____
_____
_____
_____
_____
_____
_____

Week 16

I feel like I'm showing:

- ○ A lot, like how could anyone not know I'm pregnant?
- ○ Like I've popped in the last week or 10 days.
- ○ Enough that I can tell but no one else can.
- ○ I'm breaking into maternity pants or wearing a belly band to keep my pants up.
- ○ Not really at all.

As I'm thinking about being a parent, _____ has come
to mind and I'm processing how I want to address this. My husband / partner and I have talked
about: _____
when it comes to raising you.

We agree on: _____

_____.

We are still needing to find a compromise on: _____

_____.

What I'm Thinking About This Week is: _____

_____

_____

_____

_____

_____

_____

_____

_____

_____

My Prayer / Blessing / Word for You This Week is:

My dear one, I call your spirit to attention and I bless your spirit to receive this truth over your life. I bless you to know that you were created to be a blessing and to be blessed. I bless you with the grace to receive and walk in generational blessings, whether they are passed on to you or you set a precedent and create them. I bless you to receive compliments and praise humbly and graciously so that the giver may receive the blessing of giving a blessing. I bless you to make blessing and receiving a lifestyle; that it may become your default so that it flows from the heart of God through you easily. I bless you to understand the significance and importance of blessing so that you may not only receive blessings given to you, but also realize how vital blessing others is to their lives and hearts. I bless you to be known as one who is blessed beyond belief and to live in the truth of this reality because you are a child of the King of Kings and the Lord of Lords.

Declaration for Myself / My Wife for This Pregnancy:

I declare Hebrews 4:16 over my pregnancy, which says: *"So now [I] come freely and boldly to where love is enthroned, to receive mercy's kiss and discover the grace [I] urgently need to strengthen [myself] in [my] time of weakness"* (TPT, author's emphasis). I declare that I have boldness and freedom to come to the Lord of love and to receive His mercy in the easy and the hard times. I declare that I will make new discoveries of His grace throughout this pregnancy, especially in times when I feel weak, insufficient, and inadequate. I declare I am powerful to strengthen myself in Him and in His promises when it may seem there is no hope. I likewise declare that in times of strength and hope, I will continue to be aware of and receive His grace and mercy and allow this gift to increase my hope and faith in Him to do the big things!

Week 17

I'm really starting to feel:

- ○ Huge.
- ○ Like I'm growing a baby inside.
- ○ Like I kind of wish I was showing more.
- ○ Pregnant, like it's hitting me in new ways.
- ○ Adorably, beautifully with child.

Baby, I want you to know that I really hope you _____, _____ and

_____ because I feel it's so important to your _____

_____ that you know: _____

_____.

I believe this week will be key to _____ and _____ so that

I can maintain my hope and joy regardless of circumstances. It's been a rough / great week so far.

What I'm Thinking About This Week is:_____

_____

_____

_____

_____

_____

_____

_____

_____

_____

_____

My Prayer / Blessing / Word for You This Week is:

My precious baby, I call your spirit to attention and I bless your spirit to lead your soul and body in normal growth and development right on time in every regard. I bless your spirit to know the peace of God's presence that makes impossibilities seem possible and fear no longer a thing in your thoughts or heart. I bless you to know the safety and security of knowing and walking in the depth of the peace of God. I bless you to see circumstances, people, and situations through the eyes of peace, which brings wisdom to problems; eliminates anxiety; brings rest and enjoyment to life's adventures; and ultimately takes you to a place of living in the fulfillment of Christ's promises for your life. I bless you with favor beyond measure with the Lord and with your fellow man. I bless you to be showered with favor and that everywhere your feet tread, doors are opened to you and opportunities given to you that blow people away and put them in awe of the Lord's presence in your life. I bless you with favor among men, that you don't encounter a person with whom you don't walk in favor and that this favor blesses everyone around you, not just you. I bless you with complete trust and faith in the Lord for all your days.

Declaration for Myself / My Wife for This Pregnancy:

Jeremiah 29:11 says, *"For I know the thoughts that I think toward you, says the Lord, thoughts of peace and not of evil, to give you a future and a hope"* (NKJV). I come into agreement with the truth of God's Word in this Scripture that God always has goodness to pour out on me because it's His very essence. I declare that I will live in and operate from peace and hope and belief in a GREAT future that He has for me because I choose to believe this promise He's given me. I declare this truth over every situation or aspect of my life that feels hopeless or like a dead end or impossible to solve (fill in these things that are personal for you at this time). I declare that I will not only prosper through this pregnancy but also in every other aspect of my life, which will make me a better mom too. I declare this promise for my baby's life as well, that he/she carries hope, releases hope, and lives in peace with a bright future regardless of what things may look like at any time throughout his/her life.

Did You Know?

It can be difficult to satisfy your baby's need to suck by solely nursing, (while maintaining your sanity and protecting your nipples), at least in my experience. Sucking is soothing for babies until at least six months. If you choose to introduce a pacifier, ensure a solid latch on the breast has been well-established before offering it; usually four to six weeks after birth is sufficient time. Also, ensure it doesn't become a substitute for feeding, but use it for comfort.

[Maren Wood, Postnatal Visit Conversation, 2017]

As far as decorating the baby's room goes:

- ○ I haven't really had time to think about it.
- ○ I'm starting to formulate some ideas of what I want.
- ○ I've chosen colors and/or a theme.
- ○ I'm halfway done with the room already.
- ○ Am I supposed to have gotten to this by now??

Sketch, doodle, play with lettering around some of your ideas for the baby's room here:

When it comes to your grandparents, I want you to know: _____

_____

_____

_____

As far as your uncles and aunts are concerned: _____

_____

_____

_____

What I'm Thinking About This Week is: _____

_____

_____

_____

_____

_____

_____

My Prayer / Blessing / Word for You This Week is:

Sweet one, I call your spirit to attention and I bless your spirit to hear the Word of the Lord for your life today. Exodus 14:13-14: *"Moses answered the people, 'Do not be afraid. Stand firm and you will see the deliverance the Lord will bring you today. The Egyptians you see today you will never see again. The Lord will fight for you; you need only to be still'"* (NIV). I bless you to allow God to fight your battles for you; to just sit back and rest in His favor, peace, and strength; and choose to trust his promises regardless of the circumstances. I bless you to hear, listen to, and memorize the promises God gives you both in the Scriptures as well as prophetically and in speaking daily to you so that they may become ingrained in your very being; that you may know and believe His truth and promises for your life so that you can walk into the fullness of everything God has for you in your lifetime. I bless you to lean back into His presence, His arms, especially in the hard times and to feel completely relaxed and at peace knowing that He has your back and will not let you fall. He is a good God all the time and, if He promises to fight your battles, then He'll do that every time, no questions asked. I bless these truths to sink in and be sealed in your innermost being.

Declaration for Myself / My Wife for This Pregnancy:

I declare that fear of my past issues returning during this pregnancy, or fears of what others I know have dealt with during pregnancy, will have no hold on my mind. I choose to partner with faith in God and His truth and to dwell on truth when lies or fear try to take over my thoughts. Lord, You tell us we are blessed as Your people and You direct us to bless each other and ourselves, so...I bless my spirit, soul, and body with health and strength in every regard. I bless my soul and body to line up with Your truth and the divine health You desire for me during this pregnancy and beyond into motherhood. You have only good thoughts and blessings towards me and my baby so I come into agreement with these and say yes and amen to health and wholeness and faith and hope and I refuse to agree with fear, doubt, worry or lies that You do not speak over me, in Jesus' name!

Spirit and Soul of You and Your Unborn Child

Week 19

I have felt the baby move:

- ○ A lot already, like kicks and punches.
- ○ A little, like slight touches or rolling around.
- ○ A bit, I think, like the flutters and bubbles they talk about.
- ○ Not at all yet.

I wonder how the baby is processing _____ as he/she grows. Can he/she

decipher between _____ and _____ voices?

I've noticed that baby seems to respond to _____

by moving in a certain way. I would describe it like _____

_____

_____.

I wonder what part of the body baby likes to suck most? I bet it's: Fingers / Toes / Thumb / Fist

What I'm Thinking About This Week is: _____

_____

_____

_____

_____

_____

_____

_____

_____

My Prayer / Blessing / Word for You This Week is:

My prayer for you this week and throughout your life, my sweet one, is that you would receive wisdom, revelation and value for living in the now and being present in every situation, while also having the larger vision of building towards the future. Your dad and I desire to impart legacy and inheritance to you, not only with physical resources but also with a mentality of thinking about how your choices and decisions now will affect your grandchildren, great-grandchildren, and great-great-grandchildren. We want to bless you with and teach you how to make healthy decisions and financial decisions; to be intentional with resources and your words; and to dream much larger than yourself and your lifetime so that what you leave in this world is much more profound and lasting than houses or college funds or businesses. We hope to instill in you the ability to have vision, dreams, and a purpose for future generations you will never know. We want your legacy to be a world that will forever be a different place because of how you lived your life.

Declaration for Myself / My Wife for This Pregnancy:

I bless myself with the birthright of peace in all circumstances. I bless myself with my Father's peace saturating me even in distressing circumstances. I bless myself with experiencing clearly the presence of the Holy Spirit's peace in difficult hours or days. I bless myself with feeling the peace of the presence of my Father with me and remembering to turn my affection and focus back to Him when I get distracted by the world around me. I bless myself with understanding that problems in my life are not evidence that my Father is not present with me. I bless myself with knowing that He has not and will never abandon me to my enemies. I bless myself with peace and calm of spirit and soul in spite of inconvenience or hardship, because I know that my Father is very near and that He works all things together for good. I trust Him to turn things around when it seems they are not going as I'd hoped, desired, or planned. His nearness is sweet and wonderful and good. I bless myself with honoring Him when I can't see Him with my physical eyes at work in my world. I bless myself with refusing to doubt in the dark what God has told me in the light. I bless myself with my Father's comfort when I mourn and Him giving me the oil of gladness and garments of praise in difficult times. And I declare that no matter what happens in my life during this pregnancy, I will have the grace and ability to maintain peace and not allow stress or stressful situations to hinder my health or my baby's health.

Did You Know?

There's a hormone that is released in your body during pregnancy called Relaxin. It allows the necessary parts of your body to open and move in preparation for birthing. It's not selective to only certain parts of the body however, which is why overstretching and over-exerting your body during exercise can be an issue. Stretch gently, listen to your body, and protect your joints, muscles, and bones by choosing pregnancy-specific exercise. (Eg: Pilates, walking, swimming)

[Dr. Patti Gonzalez, D.C. http://www.yourhealthelevated.com, 2016]

Week 20

The fact that I'm halfway through this pregnancy now is:

○ Not surprising, it's been great.

○ Amazing, I can't believe how fast it's gone.

○ Wow, it feels like I've been pregnant forever.

○ A relief, I think I can make it through the rest of this.

I've been wondering lately about _____.

When will _____ happen or how

will I know _____ ?

I've been experiencing joint / low back / pelvic / muscle / no pain recently. I wonder how much of it is related to *Relaxin* (the hormone) or my body adjusting to changes, and how much of it is spiritually related? (If you're feeling pain/discomfort, ask the Holy Spirit about its origination.) I feel the Holy Spirit is saying: _____

_____

_____

_____

_____.

Ask the Holy Spirit for a jingle or song to sing over your baby. Write the words here and sing it over your baby as often as you like. They love music and hearing Mommy's voice.

_____

_____

_____

_____

_____

_____

_____

What I'm Thinking About This Week is: _____

_____

_____

_____

_____

_____

_____

_____

_____

I encourage you from here on out to begin to use the appropriate pronoun or the name you've chosen as you address your baby once you've found out the gender. Or, if you've chosen to wait until your baby is born to know what you're having, insert your own pet names or whatever helps you personalize this life to aid in the bonding process and speak destiny and identity for this precious life inside of you.

For the next 10 weeks I've given you prompts for the blessings and declarations to nudge you towards making them more personalized to your specific pregnancy and detailed to what God is speaking to this child. So, go for it!

My Prayer / Blessing / Word for You This Week is:

Ask the Holy Spirit for a Scripture or talk to Him about a blessing or prophetic word He wants you to declare this week for your baby and write it down here. Declare it out loud throughout the week.

_____

_____

_____

_____

_____

_____

_____

_____

Declaration for Myself / My Wife for This Pregnancy:

Spend some time thinking about what you've been experiencing physically or in your thoughts this week that may not line up with God's best or His truth for you. Ask Him to remind you of His Word or promises in this area and write them down here as a declaration that you can speak to yourself throughout the week. _____

_____

_____

_____

_____

_____

_____

_____

_____

Love Notes

Week 21

Holy Spirit spoke to me about:

- ○ Baby's identity.
- ○ Baby's calling/gifting.
- ○ Baby's name.
- ○ My thoughts/feelings around pregnancy.
- ○ My symptoms.
- ○ Other: _____

Journal here about the details of what He spoke to you or if you haven't heard anything from Him yet, ask Him to speak to you about one of these things or something you want to know: _____

_____

_____

_____

_____

_____

_____

_____

_____

My moods lately have been _____.

I'm thankful / discouraged by this because _____

_____.

I'm going to continue moving forward with an attitude of _____

_____ and choose _____

instead of _____.

What I'm Thinking About This Week is: _____

_____

_____

_____

_____

_____

_____

_____

_____

_____

My Prayer / Blessing / Word for You This Week is:

Ask the Lord for a prayer or Scripture around releasing a blessing of obedience, integrity, and

honesty for this baby's spirit and character. Write it here: _____

_____

_____

_____

_____

_____

_____

_____

_____

_____

Declaration for Myself / My Wife for This Pregnancy:

Make a declaration for your sleep, dreams, and continued stamina for the remainder of this pregnancy. Remember, you don't have to accept what "everyone" says about negative symptoms, no sleep, discomfort, fatigue, etc. in the third trimester. Be proactive now before you enter your third trimester. _____

_____

_____

_____

_____

_____

_____

_____

_____

_____

Did You Know?

While there are varying views about breastfeeding on demand for comfort and bonding purposes, it is my experience that your baby is very good at communicating what he/she needs in this regard. Sometimes your baby is just hungry, while other times he/she needs to be cuddled and comforted at the breast. Learning how your baby communicates and being willing to fulfill his/her needs regardless of the clock and schedule can lead to an overall more settled baby, which helps Mommy remain more peaceful as well. (Refer to *The Womanly Art of Breastfeeding* for more tips on breastfeeding).

[La Leche League International, *The Womanly Art of Breastfeeding*, Seventh Revised Edition (Schaumburg, Illinois: LLLI, 2004).]

Reflections

_____

_____

_____

_____

_____

_____

_____

_____

_____

_____

_____

_____

_____

_____

_____

_____

_____

_____

_____

_____

_____

_____

_____

Week 22

Some would compare my baby to the size of a papaya this week. I think this is:

○ Very accurate.

○ Crazy, I feel WAY bigger.

○ A little disconcerting because I don't even like papaya.

○ What is a papaya and why are they comparing my baby to it?

Baby, I want so much to create a legacy for you! To me that means: _____

_____

_____

_____

_____ . I thank the Lord for grace to see this come to pass for you and your siblings.

This week I've been working on _____ for you and it's coming

along _____ .

What I'm Thinking About This Week is: _____

_____

_____

_____

_____

_____

_____

_____

_____

_____

_____

My Prayer / Blessing / Word for You This Week is:

Write down a word of hope and unity for your baby and his/her life this week. Make it something that speaks unity for every aspect of their lives and every season (unity within themselves: spirit, soul, and body; unity in relationship; unity among the body of Christ in their generation; a unity they bring to their community or places of employment etc.) Ask Holy Spirit to guide your words rather than worrying about getting it written just right. _____

_____

_____

_____

_____

_____

_____

_____

_____

Declaration for Myself / My Wife for This Pregnancy:

I bless myself / my wife with: _____

_____

_____

_____

_____

_____

_____

_____

_____

_____

I release Heaven's best for my / her pregnancy in the following areas:_____

_____

_____

_____

_____

_____

_____

_____

_____

_____

_____

_____

_____

Week 23

I'm going to go for a walk this week (at least once) and imagine what it will be like to raise a world changer (insert here what that means to you). _____

_____

_____

_____

_____

My ideas for how I can start cultivating a world-changing mindset and instilling healthy thought patterns into this child now are:

1. _____

_____

2. _____

_____

3. _____

_____

4. _____

_____

5. _____

_____

What I'm Thinking About This Week is: _____

_____

_____

_____

_____

_____

_____

My Prayer / Blessing / Word for You This Week is:

I station angels to surround you, (insert name), on all sides as you continue to develop in my womb. I bless you to become increasingly aware of the presence of the Father all around you and begin to interact with His Spirit even now. (Respond to this prompt with further declarations, or write down what Holy Spirit lays on your heart to speak to this child as you continue to press into Him with all that you are.) _____

_____

_____

_____

_____

_____

_____

Declaration for Myself / My Wife for This Pregnancy:

I plead the blood of Jesus over myself / my wife for the remainder of this pregnancy because His blood paid for my / her life to be abundant and prosperous. I declare this abundance and prosperity for (list specifics for yourself/your wife that Holy Spirit prompts whether it's difficulties you're/she's facing that should change according to the Kingdom, or things that are going well that you want to affirm and agree with).

_____

_____

_____

_____

_____

_____

_____

Did You Know?

Shannon Lane, my doula with my second son, taught me that your baby has twice the response time that you do in traumatic situations while inside the womb. For example, if someone in front of you hits their brakes hard and you react but move on within 10 seconds (heart rate slows back down etc.), it will take your baby 20 seconds. You can help facilitate a healthy ability to return to peace, from fight or flight, by talking your baby through what just happened and assuring him/her that everything is alright. This is a first step to teaching children how to regulate their nervous systems.

[Myrna Martin, video series training on "Healing Early Developmental Trauma," www.myrnamartin.net (accessed April 2020).]

Love Notes

Week 24

I wonder what your favorite _____ will be when you're 10, 15, and 22?

- ○ Sport
- ○ Hobby
- ○ Creative activity
- ○ TV show or movie
- ○ Play activity
- ○ Song

As I was working out / walking this week, I was thinking about how fun it will be to teach you about how to look after yourself in each stage of your life from _____ to _____ to _____ and _____.

Some of those specifics were: _____

_____

_____

_____

_____

What I'm Thinking About This Week is:_____

_____

_____

_____

_____

_____

_____

_____

_____

_____

_____

My Prayer / Blessing / Word for You This Week is:

Spend some time praying and making declarations for your child's future relationships (friends, parents, cousins, relatives, employers/employees, church community, spouse etc.). Pray what you hope for these relationships and how Jesus leads you to pray as you spend time with Him praying for this little one. Write any of these things here: _____

_____

_____

_____

_____

_____

_____

_____

Declaration for Myself / My Wife for This Pregnancy:

Make declarations for your spinal alignment, pelvic bones, and your body's ability to adjust well to all the movement that is required to make room for your baby to grow. Declare pain-free bodily adjustment to your bones, muscles, ligaments etc. throughout the entirety of your pregnancy. Also, declare health to your immune system and that of the baby's so that you both remain healthy and well-adapted throughout the pregnancy. Write what comes to mind, led by Holy Spirit here:

_____

_____

_____

_____

_____

_____

_____

_____

_____

Week 25

What I desire for you, my sweet baby, is:

- ○ A sweet, intimate relationship with the Lord from now through eternity.
- ○ For you to know and be known by the Lord, your family, and close friends.
- ○ For you to have a deep sense of purpose and belonging throughout your life.
- ○ To experience true joy, peace, and hope, and to encourage others with these traits.
- ○ Other _____

_____

_____

_____

Today as I thought of _____

_____

it caused me to giggle because I can just imagine you _____

_____

_____

_____

What part of nature do you imagine as you think of your baby? Do a simple sketch of that image and ask the Lord how it describes your little one. Note what He says below your sketch.

_____

_____

_____

_____

What I'm Thinking About This Week is: _____

_____

_____

_____

_____

_____

My Prayer / Blessing / Word for You This Week is:

Bless your child with the value of gratitude in his / her life, whether it's telling them what you're grateful for about them, about the Lord, or about their dad, etc. Bless them with this gift for their life in your word for them this week. _____

_____

_____

_____

_____

_____

_____

_____

_____

_____

Declaration for Myself / My Wife for This Pregnancy:

Take some time to reflect on all the parts of your pregnancy for which you can be thankful. Write your declaration from this place of gratitude towards the Lord for walking you through this pregnancy so far and thank Him in advance for what He will continue to do. _____

_____

_____

_____

_____

_____

_____

_____

Did You Know?

Your mother's intuition and instincts are invaluable. Don't ignore them for "what everyone else says you should do." There's no formula for any given situation because each baby is different. I encourage you to listen to yourself and the Holy Spirit in each parenting situation.

Reflections

_____

_____

_____

_____

_____

_____

_____

_____

_____

_____

_____

_____

_____

_____

_____

_____

_____

_____

_____

_____

_____

_____

Week 26

I'm starting to feel:

- ○ Really big.
- ○ Like I'm growing well.
- ○ I just popped this week.
- ○ Slightly uncomfortable.
- ○ Like he/she is pushing my ribs into my esophagus!

When I feel you move inside of me it makes me feel: _____

_____

_____

_____

_____

My favorite part about this sensation is: _____

_____

_____

_____

_____

Put on one of your current favorite songs and choose one or two parts of your body to move with the music (thumbs and feet or head and shoulders). Don't think too much about how you're moving. Just feel the music. Close your eyes if you need to and enjoy feeling the music inspire your movement. Make note of anything that sticks out during this movement experience. _____

_____

_____

_____

_____

_____

_____

What I'm Thinking About This Week is: _____

_____

_____

_____

_____

_____

My Prayer / Blessing / Word for You This Week is:

"For I know the thoughts that I think toward you, says the Lord, thoughts of peace and not of evil, to give you a future and a hope" (Jeremiah 29:11, NKJV). Use this Scripture...peace, a future, hope... to inspire your prayer for your little one's life this week! Go deeper than we did in Week 17 concerning your baby. _____

_____

_____

_____

_____

_____

Declaration for Myself / My Wife for This Pregnancy:

Use hope as your launch point for this week's declaration. Whether it's choosing and declaring hope when you're feeling hopeless, agreeing with the hope you're already feeling, or declaring hope over future situations around your pregnancy. Write the declaration from the hope that Jesus always offers in every situation. _____

_____

_____

_____

_____

Spirit and Soul of You and Your Unborn Child

Week 27

We're completing our second trimester together this week, my sweet one, and

- ○ I feel inspired to create beautiful things for your room.
- ○ I'm so glad to have journeyed this far with you.
- ○ I feel like there are so many things I still want to get done before you're born.
- ○ I've loved every minute and I'm excited about the next three months.

I've been pregnant for six months now and already the Lord has taught me so much about: _____

_____

_____

_____

_____

_____

_____

I've had no / a few / too many complications or scares or uncomfortable symptoms so far and I

feel: _____

_____

_____

_____

_____

_____

Thank you, Jesus, for: _____

_____

_____

_____

_____

What I'm Thinking About This Week is:_____

_____

_____

_____

_____

_____

My Prayer / Blessing / Word for You This Week is:

Give your child a mother's blessing this week, so that he/she may never suffer from the lack of one!

_____

_____

_____

_____

_____

_____

Declaration for Myself / My Wife for This Pregnancy:

If you haven't already, begin thinking about what you would like to ask the Lord for in accordance

with His good Word as part of your birth plan/story. Begin to journal declarations for your birth,

your body, your baby etc. during the labor and delivery so you know what promises you're asking

God for and choosing to focus on. _____

_____

_____

_____

_____

_____

Did You Know?

Lavender oil is the safest oil for babies and is highly effective for many things; including teething and rashes (on bottom or anywhere on their skin). In a 10 ml roller bottle, dilute 10-15 drops of lavender oil with a carrier oil such as grapeseed or fractionated coconut oil. Roll along the jawline for teething or on the affected area for rashes. Please use a separate roller bottle for the bottom area.

[Maddie Slomiany CHHCP, CNTP, CMH, CBP, http://lifehealthhappiness.com, 2017]

Love Notes

Week 28

Welcome third trimester! I counted my baby moving:

- 5-10 times daily this week.
- 10-15 times daily this week.
- 15-20 times daily this week.
- I'm not quite used to counting your movements yet.
- I didn't count but I felt you move a lot.

Someone told me recently: _____

_____

_____

_____

Initially, I thought _____

_____

_____

_____

But as I've processed these thoughts now, I'm leaning towards believing: _____

_____

_____

_____

Guess what, sweetie pie? _____

_____

_____

_____

_____

A Precious Life: A Pregnancy Journal to Nurture the

What I'm Thinking About This Week is: _____

_____

_____

_____

_____

_____

My Prayer / Blessing / Word for You This Week is:

Have your husband/partner or significant father figure in your life bless your baby with a father's

blessing, so again they may never suffer from the lack of this blessing! _____

_____

_____

_____

_____

_____

_____

Declaration for Myself / My Wife for This Pregnancy:

Make a declaration of what you want to experience in your third trimester of this pregnancy.

_____

_____

_____

_____

_____

_____

Week 29

This week, I've noticed baby has been more responsive to:

- ○ My touch.
- ○ My voice.
- ○ Music.
- ○ Daddy's voice.
- ○ Other familiar voices.
- ○ Loud sounds.
- ○ Other: _____

_____

_____

I'm trying to be more intentional about: _____

_____

_____

this week by_____,

_____,

or _____

_____.

I read _____

today / yesterday and it made me feel _____

_____

_____

_____

_____

_____

_____

A Precious Life: A Pregnancy Journal to Nurture the

If you have a life verse or specific Scripture that God's given you for this baby, use it as inspiration for creating a poem, a dance, a song, a painting, a sketch or anything else creative with your baby in mind. If you don't have a Scripture in mind, ask Holy Spirit for one. You can always use the finished product as part of the décor for baby's room. Take a picture and place it here.

What I'm Thinking About This Week is:_____

_____

_____

_____

_____

My Prayer / Blessing / Word for You This Week is:

Explore I Corinthians 2:10-11, 14-15 in light of imparting to your child the blessing and ability to live from the spirit throughout his/her life instead of primarily from the intellect and flesh. Write the blessing / revelation you receive below:_____

_____

_____

_____

_____

_____

_____

Declaration for Myself / My Wife for This Pregnancy:

The number nine represents divine completeness and the movement of God. Use this as a basis for writing a declaration for your spirit, soul, and body in trusting God to bring divine completeness to this pregnancy and trusting His movement in your life through the transition this child brings to your life. _____

_____

_____

_____

_____

_____

Did You Know?

There's an easy and safe way to disinfect and speed healing of scratches, bumps, bruises etc. as your baby grows. I received this recipe from a trusted friend who holds a certificate in French Aromatherapy with a concentration in Aromatic Medicine. It's called Children's Owie Oil: In a 10 ml roller bottle put 10 drops of Lavender, 10 drops of Tea Tree (Melaleuca) and 5 drops of Frankincense and fill the bottle with a carrier oil of your choice (Eg. grapeseed, fractionated coconut oil). I've used this on the whole family.

[Heather Johnson uses research from Robert Tisserand & Rodney Young, *Essential Oil Safety- E-book: A Guide for Health Care Professionals*, Edition 2, 2013]

Week 30

I've noticed this week that baby has been:

- ○ Extremely active.
- ○ More active than normal.
- ○ Active enough but a little more quiet than usual.
- ○ Kicking me all sorts of places I didn't realize were possible.
- ○ Other: _____

_____

_____

_____

This week I bought _____

_____

_____ for your room and I think you're going to love it!

I'm so excited to see what draws your attention in your room.

Will it be _____,

or perhaps _____,

or maybe something else I haven't even thought of yet?

What I'm Thinking About This Week is: _____

_____

_____

_____

_____

_____

_____

_____

_____

My Prayer / Blessing / Word for You This Week is:

Bless your baby's growth and development both spiritually and physically to continue to proceed normally, developing and strengthening spiritual and physical muscles needed to move in his/her calling. Explore with the Lord, as you write this blessing/prayer, what you and He desire for this child in the area of forward movement. _____

_____

_____

_____

_____

_____

_____

Declaration for Myself / My Wife for This Pregnancy:

Declare what you'd like to see in the way of forward movement or growth in your life both spiritually and physically during the rest of this pregnancy and even into the "fourth trimester" once baby has arrived. _____

_____

_____

_____

_____

_____

_____

_____

_____

At this point I will leave you to write your own blessings for your baby and declarations for yourself that are specifically catered to your needs, desires, and thoughts over the next nine weeks. Hopefully, you feel equipped enough by this stage to begin writing your own. They don't have to look a certain way, but if they come from your heart and time with the Lord, that's what counts and is significant.

We all deal with different previous traumas, fears, lies, and beliefs that can get in the way of our desired labor and delivery; or even interfere with ways to raise and pour into our children. The more of these we can tackle with the Lord by declaring what He says in place of the lies/wrong beliefs the enemy tries to convince us of, the more fullness and truth we can walk in for ourselves and our parenting. This will make our hearts feel more fulfilled and help us feel more successful as parents. I encourage you to go after these changes with the Lord in whatever capacity you feel led.

This is a time to remain continually open to what Holy Spirit wants to show you to lead you deeper into who God has created and called you to be. Just think of the legacy you can leave for your children through your own journey in this!

Reflections

Week 31

How I currently feel about bringing this little one into the world is:

○ Terrified.

○ I'm ready, let's do this thing!

○ I have some fears, but I'm working through them.

○ I'm not sure, I haven't really thought about it.

○ Today I'm feeling confident, but yesterday I was nervous.

○ Other: _____

_____

_____

I'm beginning to feel very _____

_____

_____.

But I'm trying to stay positive and think about _____

_____

_____,

instead of _____

_____

_____.

I still have _____ that I'd like to do before this little one arrives. This makes me feel

_____.

I'm choosing _____ to help me stay peaceful and

focused on what really matters.

What I'm Thinking About This Week is: _____

_____

_____

_____

_____

_____

_____

_____

My Prayer / Blessing / Word for You This Week is:

_____

_____

_____

_____

_____

_____

_____

_____

Declaration for Myself / My Wife for This Pregnancy:

_____

_____

_____

_____

_____

_____

_____

Did You Know?

There is a wonderful blend of oils that I would compare to Icy Hot®, but much cleaner, that will help soothe the muscle aches and pains of new mothers as well as anyone else. Heather calls it "Muscle Relax Oil." I do recommend using it sparingly at the start because it contains peppermint oil which has been known to decrease milk supply. Watch your milk supply carefully. Only use when necessary and discontinue use if your supply wanes or you notice any other peculiar signs of change or discomfort. You can consult an oils specialist in your area with questions.

In a 10 ml roller bottle combine 10 drops of Wintergreen, 5 drops of Lemongrass, 5 drops of Clove and 5 drops of Peppermint oil and fill with a carrier oil of your choice (Eg. grapeseed, olive, fractionated coconut oil etc.) Roll on sore muscle areas, avoiding sensitive areas (eyes, nose, vagina, nipples etc.).

[Heather Johnson uses research from Robert Tisserand & Rodney Young, *Essential Oil Safety- E-book: A Guide for Health Care Professionals*, Edition 2, 2013]

Love Notes

Week 32

It feels like this birth is:

- ○ Sneaking up on me.
- ○ Never going to arrive.
- ○ Coming sooner than expected, but I feel surprisingly ready.
- ○ Other: _____

_____

_____

We still have to buy/acquire: _____

_____

_____ before baby arrives.

We've researched _____

_____

_____

but are just having a hard time making a decision or figuring out whether we need it now or if it could wait. The baby industry is so _____.

What I'm Thinking About This Week is: _____

_____

_____

_____

_____

_____

_____

_____

_____

My Prayer / Blessing / Word for You This Week is:

_____

_____

_____

_____

_____

_____

_____

_____

Declaration for Myself / My Wife for This Pregnancy:

_____

_____

_____

_____

_____

_____

_____

_____

_____

_____

_____

Week 33

As far as a baby shower goes, we've decided to:

- ○ We already had one about _____ ago.
- ○ It's coming up in _____.
- ○ We need to make a decision about this ASAP.
- ○ We're waiting until after baby's arrival to do one.
- ○ We've decided not to do one.
- ○ Other: _____

_____

_____

_____

Something I read recently was: _____

_____

_____

_____

This fascinates me because: _____

_____

_____

_____

_____

It makes so much sense to me with regards to: _____

_____

_____

_____

_____

_____

I'm really enjoying / not enjoying reading up about _____
_____

when it comes to pregnancy / birth / baby's development / parenting / other because: _____
_____
_____
_____ .

What I'm Thinking About This Week is:

_____
_____
_____
_____
_____
_____
_____
_____
_____

My Prayer / Blessing / Word for You This Week is:

_____
_____
_____
_____
_____
_____
_____
_____

Declaration for Myself / My Wife for This Pregnancy:

_____

_____

_____

_____

_____

_____

_____

_____

_____

_____

Did You Know?

I learned from my midwife with my first son, that as your baby's saliva interacts with your mammary glands during a breastfeeding session, your body creates the needed antibodies for pathogens that your baby has been exposed to. Those antibodies are then put into your milk for your baby to receive within the same feeding. So regular breastfeeding in the mornings and evenings even when you leave bottles during work hours is crucial for your baby to receive the full immunity benefit of breastfeeding. [Maren Wood, Prenatal Conversation, 2016]

Reflections

_____

_____

_____

_____

_____

_____

_____

_____

_____

_____

_____

_____

_____

_____

_____

_____

_____

_____

_____

_____

_____

_____

_____

Week 34

This week my husband / partner said:

- ○ "You are such a sexy pregnant mama!"
- ○ "You're really growing, honey!"
- ○ "You are starting to look like a beached whale, Babe!"
- ○ Other: _____

_____

_____

_____

What he said felt _____,

and / but I know his heart is _____.

He's trying to _____

and although it may not always be eloquent, it's _____.

I'm trying to find ways to help him feel _____

because I can see he's _____.

What I'm Thinking About This Week is: _____

_____

_____

_____

_____

_____

_____

_____

_____

A Precious Life: A Pregnancy Journal to Nurture the

My Prayer / Blessing / Word for You This Week is:

_____

_____

_____

_____

_____

_____

_____

_____

Declaration for Myself / My Wife for This Pregnancy:

_____

_____

_____

_____

_____

_____

_____

_____

_____

Week 35

The nesting bug that they say is so common in pregnancy has hit me in the following ways:

- ○ I've deep-cleaned my entire house.

- ○ I've sorted through so many boxes of things from the basement and attic and gotten rid of

    _____

    _____

- ○ The baby's room is completely ready for him/her to move into.
- ○ It hasn't really hit me.
- ○ Other: _____

_____

_____

_____

_____

As I prepare for my labor and delivery, some of my thoughts are: _____

_____

_____

_____

_____

_____

_____

Some of the things I'm concerned about or have fears around are: _____

_____

_____

_____

_____

_____

_____

I think it's helpful to acknowledge these now so that I can accept they are there but choose not to focus on them. As I let go of them, I can better focus on surrendering to my birth experience and being fully: _____

_____

_____

_____

_____

What I'm Thinking About This Week is: _____

_____

_____

_____

_____

_____

_____

_____

My Prayer / Blessing / Word for You This Week is:

_____

_____

_____

_____

_____

_____

_____

_____

_____

Declaration for Myself / My Wife for This Pregnancy:

_____

_____

_____

_____

_____

_____

_____

_____

_____

_____

_____

Did You Know?

Aloe Vera can be used on your nipples to soothe them during breastfeeding. There are plenty of nipple butters and creams on the market, but you can simply buy an aloe plant, break off a small portion of a leaf and wipe the gel on your nipples after each feed.

[https://ncbi.nlm.nih.gov (accessed May 2020), Bethesda, MD: National Library of Medicine, 2018]

Love Notes

Week 36

I plan the following measures for my birth:

- Epidural all the way.
- Completely unmedicated, for sure!
- I want to try no medication, but I'm not opposed to it if I need it.
- I want to use aromatherapy, visualization, breathing, changing positions etc. to labor and work with my body.
- Other: _____

_____

_____

_____

I want to deliver this baby _____

but if complications arise, I'm processing how I feel about _____

_____

so that I feel more prepared and peaceful later if things come to that. But I'm also choosing _____

_____

_____.

Choose some of your favorite songs, both upbeat dancers and peaceful relaxers, to put in a playlist for your labor. Spend some time envisioning moving during your labor to these songs as you prepare for birth. Note any ideas or revelations the Lord gives you as you spend time doing this.

_____

_____

_____

_____

_____

What I'm Thinking About This Week is:_____

_____

_____

_____

_____

_____

My Prayer / Blessing / Word for You This Week is:

_____

_____

_____

_____

_____

_____

_____

_____

_____

Declaration for Myself / My Wife for This Pregnancy:

_____

_____

_____

_____

_____

_____

_____

_____

Week 37

Now that I'm officially at full term, I feel:

○ More than ready to bring this baby into the world.

○ Patiently ready whenever he/she is ready to come.

○ Like the major things are ready but there's more I'd still like to do before baby arrives.

○ Far from ready. I'm still running around like a crazy person.

As I sit and reflect on this pregnancy, _____

comes to mind and I feel _____

_____ .

I've decided _____

until this little one comes, because that feels most peaceful!

What I'm Thinking About This Week is: _____

_____

_____

_____

_____

_____

My Prayer / Blessing / Word for You This Week is:

_____

_____

_____

_____

_____

_____

_____

Declaration for Myself / My Wife for This Pregnancy:

_____

_____

_____

_____

_____

_____

Did You Know?

It is thought, from the minimal research done, that when your baby is ready to be born, he/she releases a hormone that triggers your hormones to start labor. Rest and allow your body to do what it was created to do.

[Condon, Jeyasuria, Faust, & Mendelson, *Nature's Plan for Birth*, 2004, nlm.nih.gov (accessed May 4, 2020)]

Week 38

We're so close and I feel:

- ○ Exhausted
- ○ Thrilled
- ○ Excited
- ○ Apprehensive
- ○ Overwhelmed
- ○ A little scared if I'm really honest.

If baby were born today, I would be / feel _____.

When I went for my prenatal checkup this week they said: _____

_____

_____

_____

Take a photograph of something that makes you smile this week and place it here. Make a statement about why this brought joy to you.

What I'm Thinking About This Week is:_____

_____

_____

_____

_____

_____

_____

_____ .

My Prayer / Blessing / Word for You This Week is:

_____

_____

_____

_____

_____

_____

_____

_____ .

Declaration for Myself / My Wife for This Pregnancy:

_____

_____

_____

_____

_____

_____

_____

Week 39

As I anticipate labor, my thoughts revolve around:

○ Fear/anxiety/pain.

○ Excitement/anticipation/joy.

○ Apprehension/mystery/uncertainty.

○ Another combination of emotions: _____

_____

_____

_____

I feel like I'm waiting for _____

_____ and yet I have no idea how to truly be prepared for what's coming.

It's like I can imagine _____

but I will have no idea what it will actually look like until it's in progress. I feel / I'm unsure _____

_____.

If you experience negative emotions this week (ie. fear, anxiety, anger) dance them out to process through and let them go. Journal about how this experience helped or affected you. (Any sort of movement can be considered dance so don't let that word stop you from gaining freedom through this exercise. As a dancer, I know it can feel like you can't dance at this stage of pregnancy; sometimes it can feel like you can barely move. But movement is important and can bring significant release of emotions).

_____

_____

_____

_____

_____

_____

_____

What I'm Thinking About This Week is:_____

_____

_____

_____

_____

_____

My Prayer / Blessing / Word for You This Week is:

_____

_____

_____

_____

_____

_____

_____

Declaration for Myself / My Wife for This Pregnancy:

_____

_____

_____

_____

_____

_____

Did You Know?

Babies' sleep cycles are much shorter than adults and they haven't yet learned how to go from one to the next seamlessly like we have. To aid them in this, you can give them some time to fuss and go back to sleep on their own rather than getting them up immediately and assuming they are hungry, or something is wrong when they make a sound. Help them learn to self-soothe early and save your sleep long term.

[Pamela Druckerman, *Bringing up Bébé: One American Mother Discovers the Wisdom of French Parenting*, (New York, NY: Penguin Group LLC, 2013) pg.38-56]

Reflections

_____

_____

_____

_____

_____

_____

_____

_____

_____

_____

_____

_____

_____

_____

_____

_____

_____

_____

_____

_____

_____

_____

Week 40

We made it to the due date!

- ○ I remember the time when I thought I'd never see this day.
- ○ It's taken forever to get here.
- ○ I'm so ready to be done with this pregnancy and on to holding my baby!
- ○ I'm celebrating the entirety of this pregnancy and eagerly awaiting the arrival of this sweet little life.
- ○ Thank you, Jesus, that we're here! I choose to trust You as we proceed!

Because I'm doing a hospital birth: _____

_____

_____

_____

_____

Since we're doing our birth at a birthing center, the procedure is: _____

_____

_____

_____

We're doing a homebirth, so: _____

_____

_____

_____

_____

No matter how things proceed, I've decided that: _____

_____

_____

_____

What I'm Thinking About This Week is:_____

_____

_____

_____

_____

_____

My Prayer / Blessing / Word for You This Week is:

_____

_____

_____

_____

_____

_____

_____

_____

Declaration for Myself / My Wife for This Pregnancy:

_____

_____

_____

_____

_____

_____

_____

_____

Reflections

_____
_____
_____
_____
_____
_____
_____
_____
_____
_____
_____
_____
_____
_____
_____
_____
_____
_____
_____
_____
_____
_____
_____
_____
_____

Reflections

_____

_____

_____

_____

_____

_____

_____

_____

_____

_____

_____

_____

_____

_____

_____

_____

_____

_____

_____

_____

_____

_____

_____

Reflections

_____

_____

_____

_____

_____

_____

_____

_____

_____

_____

_____

_____

_____

_____

_____

_____

_____

_____

_____

_____

_____

_____

Reflections

_____

_____

_____

_____

_____

_____

_____

_____

_____

_____

_____

_____

_____

_____

_____

_____

_____

_____

_____

_____

_____

_____

_____

Love Notes

Love Notes

Love Notes

Love Notes

Resources For Further Study:

Blessing Your Spirit ©2005 by Sylvia Gunter and Arthur Burk

Ministering to Babies in the Womb download from www.theslg.com/downloads

www.theslg.com See Arthur Burk's website for further resources on understanding the spirit, soul, and body and the significance of each part in who we are in Christ.

Prayers and Promises for Supernatural Childbirth ©2005 by Jackie Mize

Igniting Hope Ministries www.ignitinghope.com Steve and Wendy Backlund's teachings, books, podcasts, e-courses. (See their website and resources for further information about declarations, shifting your beliefs to God's truth, and renewing your hope about life.)

About the Author

Rebekah Lind was born in the USA and has also lived in Johannesburg, South Africa and Melbourne, Australia. She loves to travel and experience culture, whether it's language, art, customs, or sports that shape people. She holds an English Education degree and taught middle school and high school for five years before changing careers and getting back into her first love, dance. She has a heart for regional dance ministry and to see unity among dance movements across the church of Jesus Christ. This book represents the fulfillment of two life-long dreams: to write books and to be a mother. She enjoys reading, creating mixed media artwork, playing with and teaching her boys, and spending time with family and friends.

Connect with Rebekah and stay encouraged on your journey of parenting by visiting her website spiritledcreative.space.

We Want to Know What You Think!

Thank you for allowing me to be a part of this journey with you and the precious blessing God has given you. Would you do me a favor? If this book has impacted you during your pregnancy, would you please take a moment to leave a review on Amazon.com and Goodreads.com. It would also be an honor if you share this resource on any of your social media pages. My heart is to get this resource out to others who may benefit from it.

Your review does make a difference in helping other expecting families to find this resource.

CPSIA information can be obtained
at www.ICGtesting.com
Printed in the USA
FSHW021256291120
76284FS

9 781733 307864